CHURCH[ES]

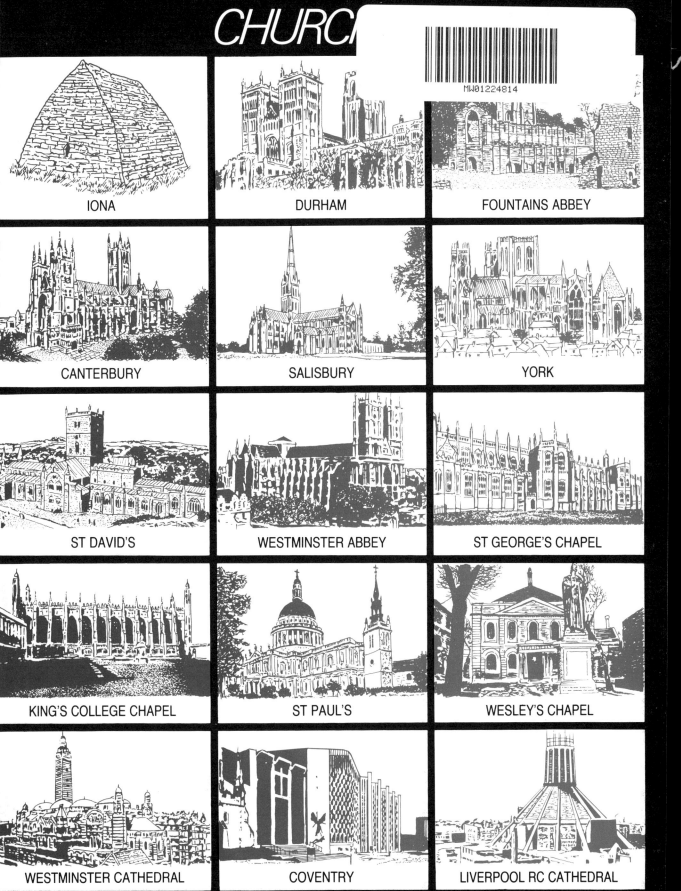

IONA

DURHAM

FOUNTAINS ABBEY

CANTERBURY

SALISBURY

YORK

ST DAVID'S

WESTMINSTER ABBEY

ST GEORGE'S CHAPEL

KING'S COLLEGE CHAPEL

ST PAUL'S

WESLEY'S CHAPEL

WESTMINSTER CATHEDRAL

COVENTRY

LIVERPOOL RC CATHEDRAL

Chiswick House was built as a temple of the arts

GREAT BRITISH
HOUSES

The Diagram Group

Franklin Watts
London New York Sydney Toronto

Acknowledgements
Picture Research: Patricia Robertson
Cover: ZEFA
Title page: Mansell Collection
BBC Hulton Picture Library 25, 29
Department of the Environment 28
Mansell Collection 12, 13, 14, 16, 18, 19 (top), 23, 27

Contents

© Diagram Visual Information Ltd 1987

First published in Great Britain 1987 by
Franklin Watts Ltd
12a Golden Square
London W1R 4BA

Printed in France

ISBN 0 86313 456 4

Building styles

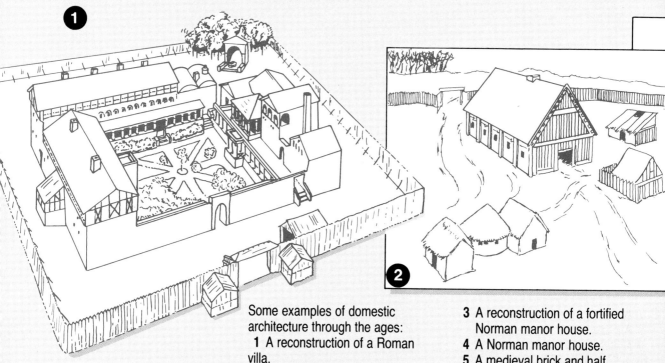

Some examples of domestic
architecture through the ages:
  1 A reconstruction of a Roman
villa.
  2 A reconstruction of a 10th-
century palace.

3 A reconstruction of a fortified
Norman manor house.
4 A Norman manor house.
5 A medieval brick and half
timber manor house.
6 A Tudor mansion.

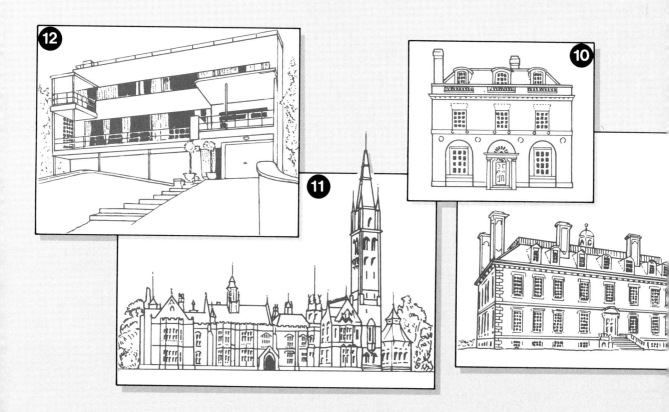

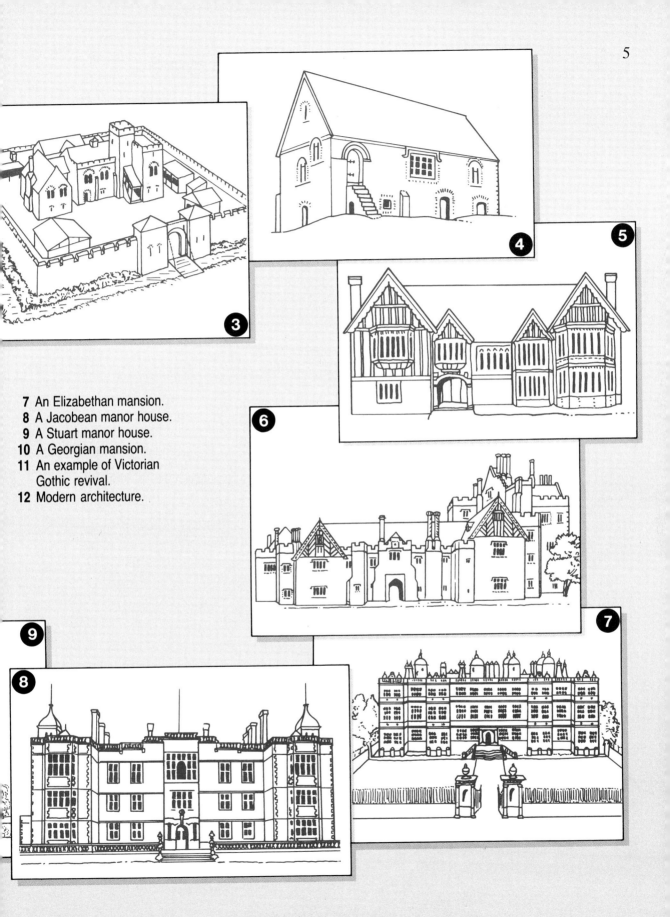

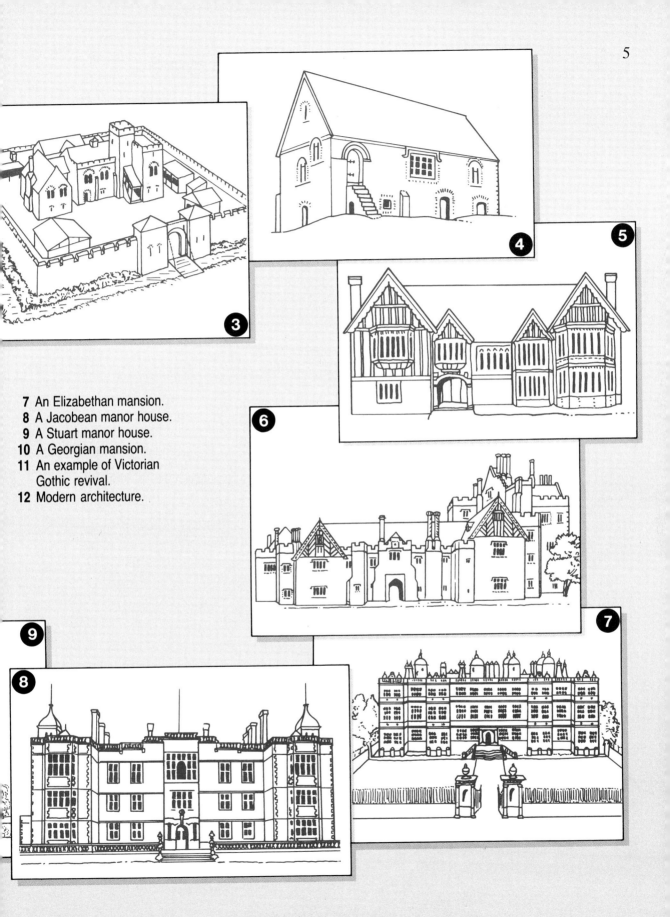

7 An Elizabethan mansion.
8 A Jacobean manor house.
9 A Stuart manor house.
10 A Georgian mansion.
11 An example of Victorian Gothic revival.
12 Modern architecture.

Woburn Abbey

The imposing West Front of the house was reconstructed by the 4th Duke of Bedford.

1145
Cistercian abbey founded
1538
Abbey confiscated by Henry VIII
1747
Rebuilding commissioned.
1802
Grounds redesigned
1841
Queen Victoria visited Woburn
1949-50
Parts of abbey demolished
1953
13th Duke inherited
1955
Woburn opened to public
1969
Extensive restoration begun

Woburn Abbey in Bedfordshire was built by Cistercian monks who came over from France in 1145. For 400 years the monks lived there until Henry VIII ordered monasteries to be shut down.

In 1547, Edward VI gave Woburn Abbey and manor to the Russell family. It was not used as a family seat until Francis Russell bought it from his cousin, the 3rd Earl of Bedford, in 1619. He became the 4th Earl of Bedford in 1627. A few alterations were made to Woburn Abbey to make it look less like a monastery.

When the 4th Duke of Bedford became the owner in 1732, parts of the abbey were falling down. He commissioned the architect, Henry Flitcroft, to rebuild the abbey in the classical style and to keep as many of the monastery buildings as possible.

The 5th Duke employed the Prince of Wales' architect, Henry Holland, to do a lot of rebuilding

in 1786. The 6th Duke was interested in gardening and asked Humphry Repton, a famous landscape gardener, to design them in 1802. His sketches are on view in the library.

In 1949, the 12th Duke had most of the 5th Duke's building pulled down, as well as part of the house which had dry rot. He was not interested in trying to restore the building. When the 13th Duke of Bedford inherited Woburn there were enormous death duties to be paid and the abbey was in a shambles. Rooms were jammed full of furniture and pictures.

He decided to open the house and grounds to the public so it would bring in some money to help with the cost of putting things right. Many of the buildings and rooms have been skilfully restored and the contents on display are some of the finest in the country.

1 The Book Room contains many rare natural history books.

2 The Grotto was designed as a covered area where the family could sit in the open. The furniture is carved to look like sea shells and dolphins. It was built facing north so was cold. Windows and doors have since been added.

3 The Deer Park has a fine collection of wild life, including nine species of deer.

4 Neil Diamond held an open air concert in 1977 in the area between the front of the house and the lake.

Hampton Court Palace

1514
Work on palace begun
1529
Wolsey left Hampton Court
1530
Henry VIII began enlarging palace
1531-36
Great Hall built
1540
Astronomical clock installed
1647
Charles I held prisoner
1689
William and Mary commissioned Wren to rebuild
1731
Further state rooms added
1768
Great vine planted
1838
State apartments and gardens opened to public free of charge

Hampton Court Palace, on the river Thames, was built by Cardinal Wolsey. He was a rich and powerful man and Lord Chancellor of England under Henry VIII. He liked to entertain on a lavish scale. He kept a household of nearly 500 people and the palace he built had 1000 rooms, all

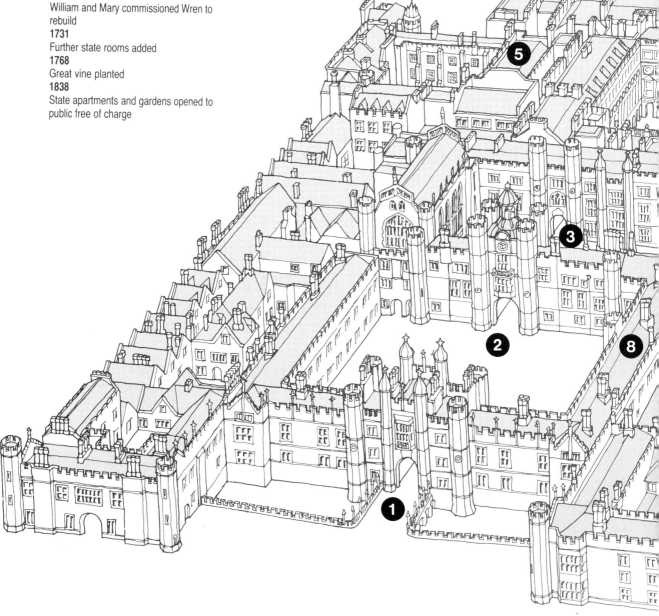

of which were used. He had rooms for 280 guests. He lived there for 15 years. When he fell out of favour with Henry VIII, he gave him Hampton Court. This was an attempt to keep the king's favour, but Cardinal Wolsey left Hampton Court in 1529 and died the following year.

Henry VIII enlarged the palace to make it one of the most splendid royal palaces. He brought all his six wives there in turn. The ghosts walking along the corridors are said to be those of Jane Seymour, who died after the birth of a son in 1537, and Catherine Howard, who was executed in 1542. They were two of Henry VIII's wives.

Charles I lived there for a while as king, and then as a prisoner for a short time during the Civil War. Oliver Cromwell used the palace and put plain glass in the chapel windows and removed pictures of the pope. Charles II repaired the palace and began landscaping the gardens.

When William and Mary moved in, in 1689, they commissioned Sir Christopher Wren to rebuild parts of the palace which was now 200 years old. The State Apartments, however, were not finished until the reign of Queen Anne. The famous maze was already planted then.

George II was the last monarch to live at Hampton Court. After that there were 50 'grace and favour' residences for widows and children of those who had given distinguished service to the crown.

The plan of Hampton Court Palace
1 The Gatehouse in the West Front
2 Base Court
3 Clock Court
4 Fountain Court
5 Chapel
6 State Apartments
7 Wolsey's rooms
8 Guests' lodgings

Beaulieu

A plan of Beaulieu showing:
1 Palace House
2 Abbey ruins
3 Miniature veteran car ride
4 Exhibition arena
5 Model railway
6 Motor Museum
7 Monorail

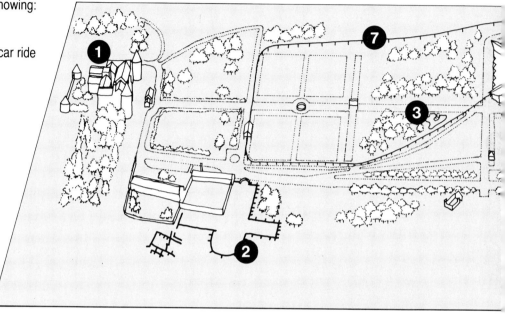

1204
Cistercian abbey founded
1500
Great Gatehouse used as reception area
1536
Abbey church pulled down
1538
Abbey seized and sold to Wriothesley
1673
1st Duke of Montagu acquired Beaulieu through marriage
1870
Gatehouse converted into family home
1951
Present Lord Montagu inherited
1952
Palace House opened to public. Motor Museum founded
1977
Monastic life exhibition opened

Palace House at Beaulieu in Hampshire was originally the Great Gatehouse of an abbey founded by 30 Cistercian monks who came from France. For 300 years, the monks had worshipped, worked, prayed, studied and farmed there. When Henry VIII closed down monasteries, some of the buildings were pulled down and the stone used for building coastal defences. The abbey and its lands were sold to Thomas Wriothesley, who later became the 1st Earl of Southampton. He was an ancestor of Lord Montagu, the present owner of Beaulieu.

The gatehouse became a family home. It had been an important part of the abbey. It was used as a reception area and the monks handed out food and clothing to the poor from there. It was modified in the 1730s by the 2nd Duke of Montagu. In 1870, it was converted and extended as a Scottish baronial manor house by Lord

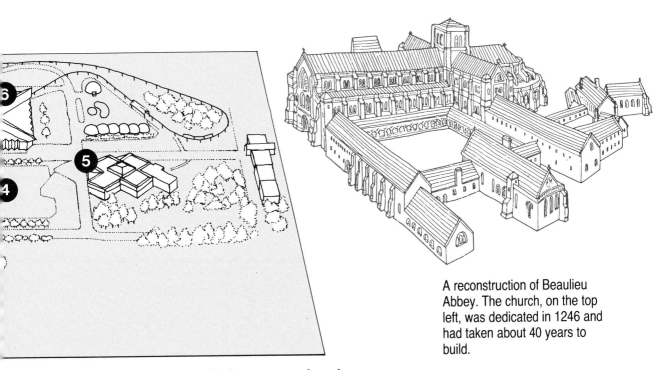

A reconstruction of Beaulieu Abbey. The church, on the top left, was dedicated in 1246 and had taken about 40 years to build.

Montagu's grandfather. It became what is now Palace House. The refectory, where the monks ate, had already become a parish church and is still in use today.

Beaulieu is perhaps best known for the National Motor Museum. Lord Montagu started this in 1952 as a memorial to his father. He began with five cars in the front hall. The exhibition now has over 200 vehicles and traces the history of the motor car from 1895.

There are also other special features at Beaulieu. There is an exhibition of life in a monastery. Some of the abbey buildings which were left standing have been beautifully restored. There are several museums and you can ride on a monorail, or in a miniature veteran car. You can also ride a 1912 London bus. There is a model railway and many radio controlled model cars with a miniature bike and car track.

This 1909 Rolls Royce Silver Ghost is in the Motor Museum. During school holidays, the veteran cars can been seen driven around the arena.

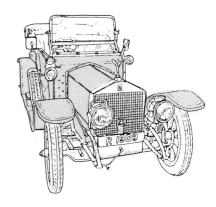

Burghley House

1158
Monastery founded on site
1539
Monastery closed down
1555-87
Burghley House built
1643
House stormed by Cromwell's troops
1775
Lake created
1789
George Rooms fitted out
1796
Grounds enlarged
1828
Corridor built round inner courtyard
1928
Lord Burghley won gold medal at Amsterdam Olympics for 400-metre hurdles

Burghley House, near Stamford in Northamptonshire, stands on the site of a 12th-century monastery. The grand Elizabethan house was built from local limestone by William Cecil. He did not employ an architect but designed the house himself. Queen Elizabeth I gave him the title Lord Burghley and made her treasurer. He was an important man so the house he built had to be suitable for someone in his position. His elder son was created Earl of Exeter and his descendents have lived at Burghley ever since.

Burghley House was planned round a courtyard, and enlarged several times. It was finished in 1587. Little remains of the inside from the Elizabethan period. The old kitchen and great hall were part of it but the rest was refurbished in the late 17th century. Originally the house had no corridors. A two-storey corridor was built round the inner courtyard in 1828. The gardens were landscaped by Lancelot 'Capability' Brown.

Many kings and queens have stayed at Burghley House. The George Rooms were prepared for George IV. He never occupied them but Queen Victoria and Prince Albert visited there. As a breakfast room, they used the Heaven Room which has gods and goddesses from ancient mythology painted all over the walls and ceilings. In contrast, the staircase outside the room is called Hell Staircase. It also has paintings by Antonio Verrio, an Italian painter, on the ceiling.

The interior of the house contains many treasures and paintings collected over the years. David Cecil, the 6th Marquess of Exeter, was a famous athlete and many of his trophies are on display.

William Cecil, the 1st Lord Burghley. He was given the title by Queen Elizabeth I and she also made him a Knight of the Garter, the highest order of chivalry in England.

The Clock Tower and Courtyard. The two-storey corridor was added to the outside of the house, making the courtyard smaller.

Longleat House

The magnificent South Front of Longleat has changed little since it was built. Wyatville replaced the front door and steps in about 1800.

1547
Building of Longleat begun
1567
Fire destroyed building, building resumed
1580
Sir John Thynne died; Longleat completed
1757-62
Grounds landscaped
1789
1st Marquess of Bath created
1801-11
Interior altered and renovated by Sir Jeffrey Wyatville
1949
Longleat opened to public by 6th Marquess of Bath
1966
First safari park opened

In 1540, Sir John Thynne bought the Longleat property in Wiltshire. The estate was once the site of a late 13th-century Augustinian priory. It was named after the long 'leat' or stream running through it. Sir John Thynne designed the house himself, and he organised the materials needed to built it. There were setbacks. In 1567 fire raged through the half-finished structure, but he started building again. When Sir John died in 1580, Longleat was completed. It has remained in the same family ever since.

The exterior of the house has changed little but inside only the Great Hall remains almost as Elizabethan craftsmen created it. Over 400 years many renovations and improvements have been made. Ornate ceilings were created, and furniture and paintings suitable for royal visitors were bought. The park was landscaped by Lancelot 'Capability' Brown. It was expensive to run the house and estate. One owner is said to have asked his tenants for 20 years' rent in advance to pay for alterations.

The 6th Marquess of Bath and Jimmy Chipperfield agreed in 1964 to bring the lions to Longleat. For 6 months, while the lions were in quarantine, Chipperfield's zoos seemed to be full of only lions.

The Safari Park has many other animals, including giraffes, gorillas and rhinoceroses.

After the Second World War, the house was opened to the public by the 6th Marquess of Bath. Public contributions were needed to help maintain and preserve the house. However, this did not bring in enough money. With the help of Jimmy Chipperfield, the Marquess decided to bring in lions and to open a safari park at Longleat. There was much public protest about having lions running loose on the estate but it proved to be a great success. Since then many other wild animals from all over the world have been added. In contrast, there is also a pets' corner with tame animals so children can get close to them.

Hatfield House

The imposing South Front of Hatfield House. The main entrance is on the north side.

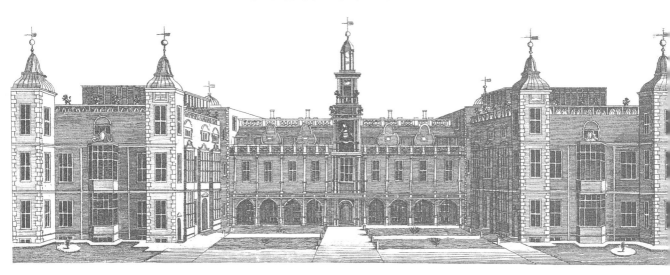

Queen Elizabeth I in about 1547, when she was still a princess.

The history of Hatfield House in Hertfordshire began about 1497. It was built by Cardinal Morton, minister of Henry VII. When Henry VIII shut down monasteries and took away church property, he took the Old Palace over and used it for his children. Elizabeth I spent much of her childhood here and even held her first Council of State in 1558 at Hatfield.

James I, Queen Elizabeth I's successor, did not like the Old Palace and exchanged it for Theobalds. This was owned by Robert Cecil, later lst Earl of Salisbury. He was the son of William Cecil who built Burghley House. Hatfield House has been the home of the Cecil family ever since.

Robert Cecil pulled down three sides of the Old Palace and used the bricks to build Hatfield House. He died in 1612, before the house was finished. The house is Jacobean and follows a

design popular in Elizabethan times. A central block joins two wings, forming the letter E, for the queen's initial.

There was a fire in 1835 and the first Marchioness of Salisbury died. The fire engines had to come from London, 21 miles away. The inside of the west wing was mostly destroyed. The chapel survived because the fire melted the leaden water tanks on the roof. The wind also changed and it began to snow. Her son, the 2nd Marquess, rebuilt the house and restored the Elizabethan-style decorations.

One of the outstanding features of Hatfield House is the long gallery. No great house was considered complete without one, and Robert Cecil made it as long as he could. It runs the whole length of the south front. There are mementoes of Elizabeth I there.

The Marble Hall was once used as a dining room. It has a minstrels' gallery and takes up two floors of the house. The floor is the original black and white marble.

c1497
Old Palace completed
1558
Queen Elizabeth I held first Council of State at Hatfield
1607
James I changed houses with Robert Cecil for Theobalds Manor
1608-12
Present Hatfield House built
1835
Fire damaged house. 1st Marchioness of Salisbury died
1881
Electric lighting installed
1900
Gardens restored

The Palace of Holyroodhouse

The Palace of Holyroodhouse is at the end of the Royal Mile leading down from Edinburgh Castle in Scotland. According to legend, King David I chose this beautiful spot after he had a vision of the Holy Cross (Rood). He ordered an abbey to be built there.

At first, Holyroodhouse was little more than a guesthouse. King James IV and his son, James V, enlarged the royal apartments. When Mary Queen of Scots came to Holyroodhouse, the monastery no longer existed. After the murder of David Rizzio, she left Holyroodhouse in 1566. Her son, James VI, came to live there in 1578. He left in 1603 when he also became King James I of England. There were no royal occupants for 200 years.

After the execution of Charles I during the Civil War, Oliver Cromwell and his troops stayed at Holyroodhouse. Fire damaged the palace and some of it was repaired. When Charles II became king, he ordered a new palace to be built in the classic Renaissance style that we see today.

In 1745, Bonnie Prince Charlie, Prince Charles Edward Stuart, lodged there before his invasion of England when he was trying to restore the Stuarts to the throne.

George IV was the first reigning monarch to visit Scotland since Charles I. He paid a state visit to Holyroodhouse in 1822 and the house regained some of its former splendour. Queen Victoria often stayed there on her way to Balmoral Castle and improved the furnishing and made the palace a royal residence. It is now the Queen's offical residence in Scotland. The Queen and Prince Philip spend three weeks there every summer.

Mary Queen of Scots married Henry Stuart, Lord Darnley at Holyrood Abbey. She was later suspected of his murder.

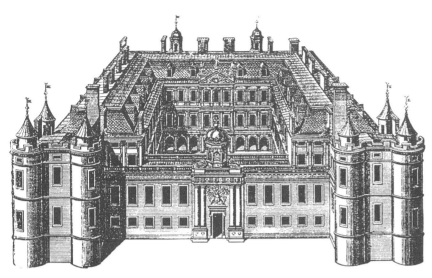

The West Front of Holyroodhouse. The James IV Tower, on the left, was built in 1529-32. The tower on the right was added between 1671-80.

The Queen's bedchamber through which David Rizzio, her Italian secretary, was dragged. He was stabbed 59 times by Lord Darnley's men. The blood stains are marked by a brass plaque on the floor.

Castle Howard

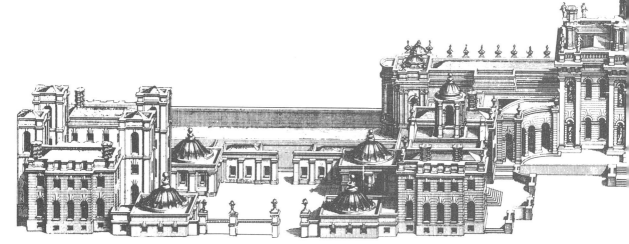

The Temple of the Four Winds. This was the last of Sir John Vanbrugh's works.

1700
Work on Castle Howard began
1724-26
Temple of the Four Winds designed by Vanbrugh
1726
Vanbrugh died
1731
Work on Mausoleum began
1738
3rd Earl of Carlisle died

Castle Howard in North Yorkshire stands on the site of Henderskelfe Castle which was gutted by fire in 1693. Charles Howard, 3rd Earl of Carlisle, commissioned John Vanbrugh to design the house. Vanbrugh had been a soldier and written plays, but this was the first house he designed. He worked with the architect Nicholas Hawksmoor.

Castle Howard was the first private house to be built with a dome. The design of the house changed several times as it was being built. This was very common in those days. The building took a long time because Lord Carlisle never had enough money to do all he wanted. Vanbrugh died in 1726 before the building was finished. After Hawksmoor died, Sir Thomas Robinson, who was married to Lord Carlisle's daughter, took over the building.

When the 3rd Earl died, Robinson persuaded his son, the 4th Earl of Carlisle, to allow him to carry on the work. He destroyed some of Vanbrugh's work and built a new wing. He planned to make more changes but the 4th Earl died before these could be done. The 5th Earl was

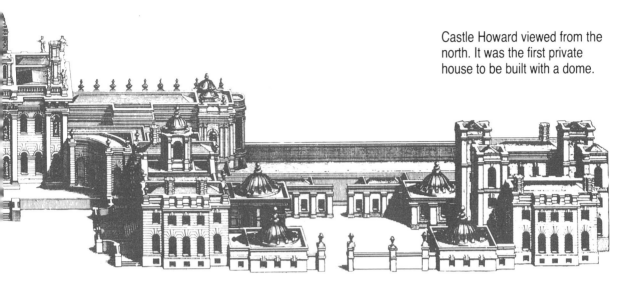

Castle Howard viewed from the north. It was the first private house to be built with a dome.

only ten years old when he succeeded to the title and his trustees did little work on the house. In about 1800, he had the interior of the wing finished. Further alterations were carried out by successive earls.

In 1940, during the Second World War, the house was used as a girls' school. There was a fire which damaged the dome and roof but these have been repaired. The house and grounds were reopened to the public in 1952. The famous collections of pictures and fine furniture are all on display along with other treasures. Restoration of the house and buildings was started then and still continues today.

The Mausoleum was designed by Hawksmoor but he did not live to see it finished. The 3rd Earl of Carlisle, who built Castle Howard, is buried there.

1753-59
West wing built by Robinson
1870-75
Chapel refitted
1940
Central dome damaged by fire
1952
House reopened to public

Blenheim Palace

Blenheim Palace in Oxfordshire was built for John Churchill, 1st Duke of Marlborough. He was given the manor, and some money to build it with, by Queen Anne as a reward for his victory over the French at the Battle of Blenheim in 1704. Building of the palace began in 1705.

It was designed in the Baroque style by Sir John Vanbrugh, who again asked Nicholas Hawksmoor to work with him. Building stopped in 1712 when the Duke and Duchess of Marlborough left England after falling from favour with Queen Anne. They returned after she died and building began again in 1716.

A great architectural achievement was the Grand Bridge. Vanbrugh planned this to have rooms in it but the Duchess disagreed. The Duchess found fault with everything Vanbrugh

The silver centrepiece of the Duke of Marlborough after the victory at the Battle of Blenheim. He is still on horseback writing a despatch to his duchess.

Sir Winston Churchill, who was born at Blenheim in 1874.

planned because she had wanted Sir Christopher Wren to design the house. After an argument with her, Vanbrugh left in 1716. The Triumphal Arch, by Nicholas Hawksmoor, was raised in 1723 after the Duke had died. The building of Blenheim Palace was finally finished in 1725, and the Column of Victory, with the statue of the Duke, was completed in 1730. Lancelot 'Capability' Brown was asked to landscape the gardens.

Among the rooms open to the public is the one in which Sir Winston Churchill was born. The exhibits include many of his personal books and photographs. There are also outstanding collections of tapestries, paintings, sculptures and furniture in the state rooms. The Long Library has over 10,000 books. The house is set in beautiful gardens with formal water terraces with fountains, a cascade and less formal pleasure grounds. There is also a narrow gauge railway which runs between the palace and Garden Centre.

The North Front of Blenheim with the Great Court. There are many stone carvings by Grinling Gibbons on the buildings. He was a famous sculptor.

Among the many personal exhibits of Sir Winston Churchill are these curls which were cut when he was five years old.

Broadlands

The original manor of Broadlands, on the River Test in Hampshire, was owned by Romsey Abbey, which was closed down by Henry VIII. It had several private owners and, in 1736, Henry Temple, the 1st Viscount Palmerston, bought the manor and started work on the gardens. The 2nd Viscount Palmerston altered the house to make it into the Palladian mansion that we see today. The gardens were landscaped by Lancelot 'Capability' Brown.

The 3rd Viscount Palmerston, Henry John Temple, became prime minister in the reign of Queen Victoria. When he died, the house was owned by his stepson, and passed from a nephew to his son. This was Wilfred Ashley, Lord Mount Temple. He died in 1939 and his daughter, Edwina, inherited the house. She had married Lord Louis Mountbatten in 1922 and they had spent their honeymoon at Broadlands.

Lady Mountbatten took great care to keep the 18th-century elegance of the house. She was an

The transformation into an elegant Palladian mansion began in 1767. The approach to the river was also altered then to give a gentle descent.

Broadlands has been a favourite place for royal couples to start their honeymoon. The Queen and Prince Philip began theirs at

Broadlands in 1947. The Prince and Princess of Wales also began theirs at Broadlands in 1981.

important hostess and many distinguished visitors stayed there. During the Second World War, Broadlands was used as a hospital annexe. The moulded walls and book cases were boarded up but patients could still gaze up at the magnificent ceilings.

Lord Mountbatten opened his home to the public only four months before he was assassinated off the coast of Ireland in 1979. His family decided that the best monument to him and his life would be to carry on his wishes and create the Mountbatten Exhibition. It includes an audio-visual film which illustrates the brilliant career of a man who was a sailor, commander, statesman and diplomat, and of his wife who was with him on many triumphal occasions. Also included are the uniforms, decorations, trophies and gifts he received.

Admiral of the Fleet, the Earl Mountbatten of Burma, after the painting of him at Broadlands.

Chiswick House

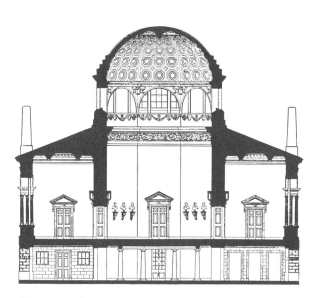

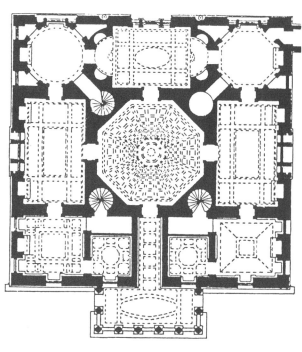

A cross section and first floor plan showing the layout of Chiswick House.

1682
1st Earl of Burlington bought Chiswick property
1725-29
Chiswick Villa built
1736
Inigo Jones gateway installed
1753
Estate passed to Duke of Devonshire
1788
Mansion demolished, villa enlarged
1892
Art treasures removed to Chatsworth; property used as mental home
1919
Estate sold to county council
1952
Side wings demolished

The 1st Earl of Burlington bought the mansion and estate at Chiswick because he wanted a country place which was convenient to London. It now is part of London. He enlarged the mansion but it was his grandson, Richard Boyle, the 3rd Earl of Burlington, who built the villa, as it was then called. Lord Burlington modelled his villa on one designed by the Italian architect, Andrea Palladio, which he had seen and liked on his travels in Italy.

The villa was not intended as a residence. Lord Burlington still lived in the mansion and became a great patron of the arts. He wanted a temple of the arts where he could meet his friends, and a gallery where he could display the works of art he had collected. Chiswick Villa looked like an ancient Roman temple, with columns and an octagonal (eight-sided) dome. The interior

decoration was based on designs by Inigo Jones.

After Lord Burlington died, the estate passed to the Duke of Devonshire. The 5th Duke pulled down the mansion and made the villa larger. He added wings on the north and south. The house remained a great social centre and many important visitors were entertained there. Among these were the Tsars of Russia. In 1892, the 8th Duke moved some of the treasures to Chatsworth House and Chiswick House was used as a lunatic asylum for a while.

In 1929, Middlesex County Council bought the estate and the grounds were opened as a public park. In 1952 the wings which had been added were found to be beyond repair and had to be pulled down. The house and gardens are now under the care of English Heritage who look after many historic buildings and monuments.

Chiswick House was built as a classic temple of the arts, not as a residence.

The Inigo Jones gateway was originally at Beaufort House in Chelsea. It was brought to Chiswick in 1736.

10 Downing Street

The house, which was once two houses, has the most famous and most photographed front door.

1683
Development of street begun
1723-35
Two houses made into one
1825
Alterations begun by John Soane
1902
A. J. Balfour began tradition of prime ministers to live there
1937
State rooms refurbished
1939-45
House damaged by bombs
1955
Sir Winston Churchill retired
1960-63
House vacated for major repairs
1979
Margaret Thatcher became first woman prime minister

Number 10 Downing Street probably has the best-known front door in Britain. As the entrance to the official home of the prime minister, it is one of the most used. When a doorkeeper ran a check on one day's comings and goings in the 1960s, the famous front door was opened 945 times between 6am and 11pm. In fact, this door is so highly regarded that a replica of it is kept in store in case it is ever needed.

The front door opens onto numerous staircases and corridors. The house contains both official rooms, like the Cabinet Room, and private apartments for the prime minister. The walls on the staircase are hung with portraits of all the prime ministers.

Number 10 was originally two houses which faced onto St James's Park. When they were combined, the front became the back and the Downing Street entrance became the front. It was

first used as an official residence by Sir Robert Walpole. After he resigned, it was not used as an official home for 20 years.

It was not until A. J. Balfour's time at the beginning of this century that the tradition was established of the prime minister taking up official residence at Number 10. Every prime minister has lived there since, except Harold Wilson (now Lord Wilson) in his second term of office (1974-76).

The position of the house is one reason why it has become so important. It is surrounded by government buildings, like the Treasury and Foreign Office. Number 11 is where the Chancellor of the Exchequer lives, and there is even a connecting door between Number 10 and 11. Number 12 is the Chief Whip's office, and the Houses of Parliament are only a few hundred yards away.

1 Sir Winston Churchill was one of the famous residents at Number 10. He lived there from 1940-45 and 1951-55.

2 Margaret Thatcher, the first woman prime minister in Britain, outside Number 10 Downing Street, her official residence.

Harewood House

The North Front of Harewood House. The house was open to visitors in the 18th and 19th centuries, but only by appointment with the butler or housekeeper.

1738
Site purchased by Lascelles family
1759
Foundations laid
1765
Exterior completed
1771
Harewood House habitable
1772-81
Gardens landscaped
1843
Major alterations begun
1950
Harewood opened to public
1962
Storms destroyed 20,000 trees
1970
Bird Garden established
1972
Education Centre opened
1975
Adventure playground built

Edwin Lascelles began building Harewood House in Yorkshire in 1759. He had inherited the estate from his father, who had made his money in the West Indies. It has been the family home ever since.

Edwin wanted a Palladian house so he commissioned John Carr of York to draw up the plans and adapt the 16th-century style of Italian Andrea Palladio to 18th-century English. The exterior of the house was finished six years after the foundations were laid. He then asked the brilliant architect and designer, Robert Adam, to design the interior. He also commissioned Thomas Chippendale to make all the furniture and Lancelot 'Capability' Brown to landscape the grounds. Edwin Lascelles became the 1st Lord Harewood in 1790. He died five years later.

No major changes were made to the house until 1843. The 3rd Earl had married Lady Louisa Thynne from Longleat. She found the house

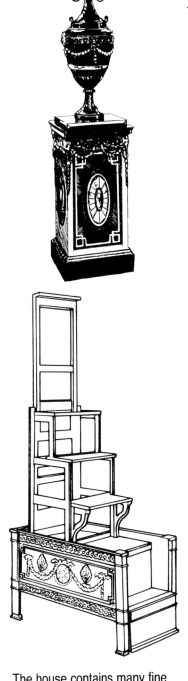

The Bird Garden at Harewood has over 8,600 different kinds of birds.

inconvenient and asked Sir Charles Barry to add a third storey to the house. He had designed the new Houses of Parliament. When the 4th and 5th Earls owned the house, modern heating, gas and electricity were installed.

It was the 6th Earl who added many art treasures to the house. He had inherited money and paintings from his great-uncle and so started his own collection. He married Princess Mary, daughter of George V and later Princess Royal, in 1922. They did much restoration work on the house which had been used as a convalescent hospital during the First World War.

When the 6th Earl died, there were large estate duties to be paid. Land was sold to raise money and the house was opened to the public three years later.

The house contains many fine examples of furniture. There is an Adams-Chippendale silver chest and wine cooler, and an elaborate piece covered in red leather. It was made by Chippendale. When the top is lifted, it shows folding library steps.

Royal Pavilion, Brighton

A cut-out of the Royal Pavilion. The Saloon, on the right under the big dome, was the only room left of the original Marine Pavilion.

1783
Prince of Wales first went to Brighton (Brighthelmstone)
1787
Marine Pavilion built by Henry Holland
1811
Prince became Prince Regent
1815
Nash began creating Royal Pavilion
1820
Prince Regent became George IV
1827
George IV's last visit
1830
George IV died at Windsor
1850
Royal Pavilion sold to Brighton by Queen Victoria
1975
Music Room damaged by fire
1982
Restoration begun

Until the 19th century, Brighton was called Brighthelmstone. It was a small fishing village on the south coast. The Prince of Wales, later George IV, first went there in 1783. He entertained many friends and it soon became fashionable. Sea water was thought to be good for the health, both for drinking and bathing. In those days, wealthy people ate too much and did not wash very often.

After his father, George III, became too ill, the Prince of Wales became Prince Regent and took over his father's duties as king. The Marine Pavilion, which had been built for him by Henry Holland, became too small. He asked the architect John Nash to enlarge the building.

The simple villa was transformed into the magnificent palace that we see today. It became an oriental fantasy with Indian-style domes and minarets on the outside. The inside has Chinese-style decorations and a lot of bamboo furniture. The music room has paintings in red and gold of

33

The magnificent East Front showing the domes and minarets.

flying dragons and other imaginary creatures. The Banqueting Room has a carved flying dragon with huge plantain leaves. The centre lighting hangs from it. There were seldom fewer than 30 or 40 guests at a banquet. The Prince entertained lavishly. One menu in 1817 listed 112 dishes. When he died at the age of 67, he weighed 23 stone.

William IV, who succeeded his brother, had been a naval officer and liked Brighton because it was by the sea. He used the Pavilion during his seven-year reign. Queen Victoria, however, found Brighton too crowded and she abandoned the Pavilion in 1845. It was bought by the town five years later. Since then it has been very carefully restored.

George IV, when he was still Prince Regent. He had the Royal Pavilion built when he needed more space for formal duties.

Buckingham Palace

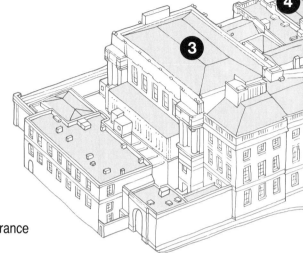

The buildings that make up Buckingham Palace. The East Front with the central balcony is the well-known view. The State Apartments are on the West Front, overlooking the gardens. The first floor of the north wing has the Private Apartments.

1 Central balcony
2 Ambassador's entrance
3 Ballroom
4 State Dining Room
5 Music Room
6 Throne Room
7 Garden Entrance
8 Chinese Luncheon Room

Buckingham Palace in London is the most famous residence in the world. For a royal palace, it is not really very old. Until 1831, it was known as Buckingham House. George III had bought the house in 1761 and lived in it with his family for many years. It was a private residence. The court remained at St James's Palace.

George IV asked the architect John Nash to convert the house, but he did not live to see it completed. He had planned to hold court there. His brother, William IV, did not like the palace and offered it to the government after the Houses of Parliament burned down in 1834. His offer was turned down.

Queen Victoria was the first monarch to live and hold court there. She moved there in 1837 at the age of 18. The royal standard to show when she was in residence was flown from the top of

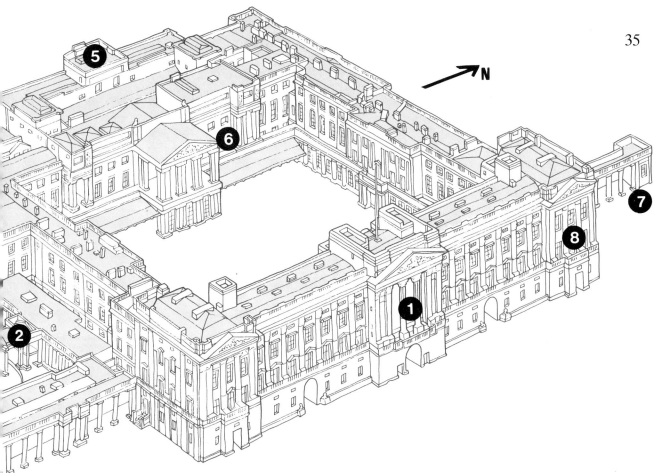

Marble Arch. It then stood at the entrance to the forecourt, but was moved to the north-east corner of Hyde Park. Nash had always said that the palace was too small for a state palace. In 1847 Edward Blore added the East Front. The royal standard now flies from the roof immediately above the central balcony of this. It is the famous balcony where the Royal Family stands to wave to the crowds outside. It was first used by Queen Victoria in 1854 to watch the soldiers leaving for battle in the Crimea. It had been newly built then.

In 1854, Sir James Pennethorne, who had studied under Nash, made alterations to provide for the Ball Room. Thousands of people go there by invitation to banquets and investitures, and they go to garden parties but the only parts of the palace open to the public are the Royal Mews and the Queen's Gallery.

1761
George III bought Buckingham House
1825
John Nash began transformation of house to palace
1831-37
Blore completed work
1837
Queen Victoria moved in
1853-55
Ball Room constructed
1911
Victoria memorial unveiled
1913
Alterations made to palace
1940
Palace bombed, chapel wrecked
1961
Queen's Gallery opened
1963
Guard-mounting ceremony moved from St James's Palace
1970
Exterior cleaned

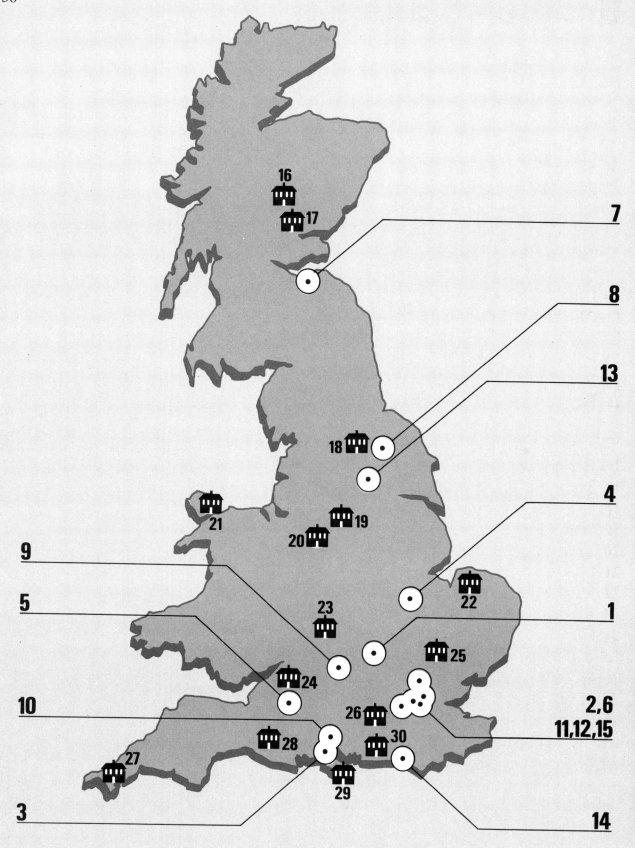

7

8

13

4

1

9

5

10

2,6
11,12,15

3

14

16

17

18

19

20

21

22

23

24

25

26

27

28

29

30

Houses of interest

The houses in this book
1 Woburn Abbey, Bedfordshire
2 Hampton Court Palace, Surrey
3 Beaulieu, Hampshire
4 Burghley House, Stamford, Lincolnshire
5 Longleat House, Warminster, Wiltshire
6 Hatfield House, Hertfordshire
7 The Palace of Holyroodhouse, Edinburgh, Lothian
8 Castle Howard, Yorkshire
9 Blenheim Palace, Woodstock, Oxfordshire
10 Broadlands, Romsey, Hampshire
11 Chiswick House, London
12 10 Downing Street, London
13 Harewood House, Yorkshire
14 Royal Pavilion, Brighton, Sussex
15 Buckingham Palace, London

Some other interesting houses
16 Blair Castle, Blair Atholl, Tayside
17 Scone Palace, Perth, Tayside
18 Newby Hall, Ripon, North Yorkshire
19 Chatsworth House, Derbyshire
20 Little Moreton Hall, Congleton, Cheshire
21 Plas Newydd, Isle of Anglesey, Gwynedd
22 Sandringham House, Norfolk
23 Ragley Hall, Alcester, Warwickshire
24 Claverton Manor, Bath, Avon
25 Knebworth House, Hertfordshire
26 Stratfield Saye House, near Reading, Hampshire
27 St Michael's Mount, Cornwall
28 Parnham, Beaminster, Dorset
29 Osborne House, Isle of Wight
30 Goodwood House, near Chichester, West Sussex

Things to look for in a house

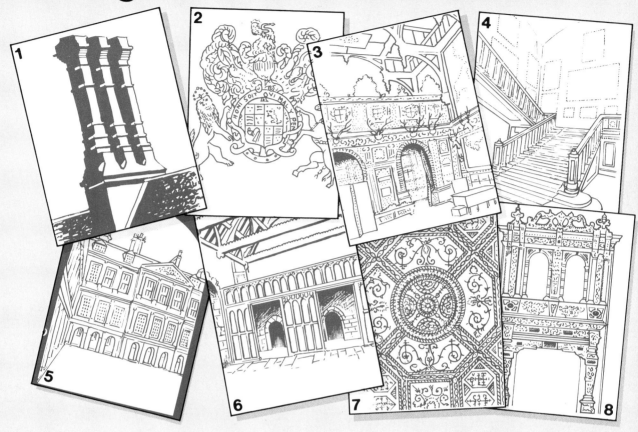

1 Chimneys Brick chimneys came into use early in the 16th century. Some were very elaborate and gave bricklayers a chance to show off their skills.

2 Coat of arms This is the heraldic emblem of a family or a person. They are often displayed above doorways or sometimes modelled into ceilings.

3 Minstrels' gallery This was a balcony, usually in the great hall, where the minstrels or wandering musicians entertained at parties.

4 Grand staircase All great houses have a grand staircase in the great entrance hall. There is usually a much smaller staircase hidden away, which the servants used.

5 Courtyard Many great houses have a private open area which is completely surrounded by buildings. It cannot be overlooked from outside.

6 Panelled screens These were panels usually covering walls. They were made of wood and often very elaborately carved.

7 Decorative ceilings Many houses have very ornate ceilings, often with a geometrical pattern picked out in different colours so you can see the mouldings.

8 Ornamental fireplaces These are often great works of craftsmanship with elaborate carvings and designs. They are usually carved from wood, marble or stone.

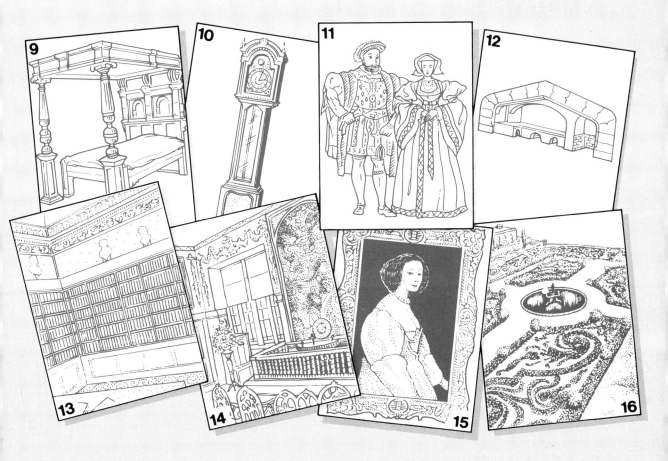

9 Four-poster bed Large bedrooms were needed for these beds. They often had very elaborate carvings on the supports and canopies, and curtains which could be pulled all round.

10 Grandfather clock There are many grandfather clocks in the great houses. They often have chimes and ornately carved cases.

11 Period costumes Clothes from all ages are on display in great houses. These are early Tudor costumes.

12 Kitchen ovens This is the kind of Tudor oven which can be found at Hampton Court Palace. They were huge as they had to cook food for many people at the same time.

13 Library All great houses have a library. Some have very fine collections of books with rare copies.

14 Family chapel Most great houses had a chapel joined on to the house where all the family could pray and worship.

15 Family portraits Most houses have portraits of people who lived there. Artists were hired specially to paint them.

16 Formal gardens Many houses have gardens which were specially designed and landscaped where the family could go for walks. They require a lot of work to keep them attractive at all times.

Useful addresses

English Heritage
PO Box 43
Ruislip
Middlesex HA4 0XW
(Historic Buildings and Monuments Commission)
(Written enquiries only)

The National Trust
(for Places of Historic Interest or Natural Beauty)
36 Queen Anne's Gate
London SW1H 9AS
Tel: 01 222 9251

Society for the Protection of Ancient Buildings
37 Spital Square
London E1 6DY
Tel: 01 377 1644

English Tourist Board
4 Grosvenor Gardens
London SW1W 0DJ
Tel: 01 730 3400

Scottish Tourist Board
23 Ravelston Terrace
Edinburgh EH4 3EU
Tel: 031 332 2433

National Trust for Scotland
5 Charlotte Square
Edinburgh EH2 4DU
Tel: 031 226 5922

CADW Welsh Historic Monuments/Wales Tourist Board
Brunel House
2 Fitzalan Road
Cardiff CF2 1UY
Tel: 0222 499909

Northern Ireland Tourist Board
River House
48 High Street
Belfast BT1 2DS
Tel: 0232 231221

Historic Houses Association
38 Ebury Street
London SW1W 0LU
Tel: 01 730 9419

Index

HOUSES

WOBURN

HAMPTON COURT

BEAULIEU

BURGHLEY

LONGLEAT

HATFIELD

HOLYROODHOUSE

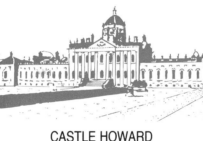

CASTLE HOWARD

BLENHEIM

BROADLANDS

CHISWICK

10 DOWNING STREET

HAREWOOD

ROYAL PAVILION

BUCKINGHAM PALACE